VALENTINE'S DAY

by Charly Haley

Cody Koala

An Imprint of Pop!
popbooksonline.com

abdobooks.com
Published by Pop!, a division of ABDO, PO Box 398166, Minneapolis, Minnesota 55439. Copyright © 2019 by POP, LLC. International copyrights reserved in all countries. No part of this book may be reproduced in any form without written permission from the publisher. Pop!™ is a trademark and logo of POP, LLC.

Printed in the United States of America, North Mankato, Minnesota

082018
012019

THIS BOOK CONTAINS RECYCLED MATERIALS

Cover Photo: Shutterstock Images
Interior Photos: Shutterstock Images, 1, 5 (bottom left), 7, 13, 15, 16, 20, 21; iStockphoto, 5 (top), 5 (bottom right), 9, 10, 19 (top), 19 (bottom left), 19 (bottom right)

Editor: Meg Gaertner
Series Designer: Laura Mitchell

Library of Congress Control Number: 2018949240
Publisher's Cataloging-in-Publication Data
Names: Haley, Charly, author.
Title: Valentine's day / by Charly Haley.
Description: Minneapolis, Minnesota : Pop!, 2019 | Series: Holidays | Includes online resources and index.
Identifiers: ISBN 9781532162015 (lib. bdg.) | ISBN 9781641855723 (pbk) | ISBN 9781532163074 (ebook)
Subjects: LCSH: Valentine's day--Juvenile literature. | Holidays--Juvenile literature. | Saint Valentine's Day--Juvenile literature.
Classification: DDC 394.2618--dc23

Hello! My name is
Cody Koala

Pop open this book and you'll find QR codes like this one, loaded with information, so you can learn even more!

Scan this code* and others like it while you read, or visit the website below to make this book pop.

popbooksonline.com/valentines-day

*Scanning QR codes requires a web-enabled smart device with a QR code reader app and a camera.

Table of Contents

Chapter 1
Valentine's Day 4

Chapter 2
Secret Love 8

Chapter 3
St. Valentine 14

Chapter 4
Celebrations 18

Making Connections 22
Glossary. 23
Index 24
Online Resources 24

Chapter 1

Valentine's Day

People are sharing paper cards and candy hearts. They are spending time with the people they love. It is Valentine's Day.

Watch a video here!

Valentine's Day happens each year on February 14. It is a day to celebrate love.

> You can celebrate Valentine's Day with your friends, family, or classmates.

February

Mon	Tue	Wed	Thu	Fri	Sat	Sun
						1
2	3	4	5	6	7	8
9	10	11	12	13	14	15
16	17	18	19	20	21	22
23	24	25	26	27	28	

Chapter 2

Secret Love

The holiday began in **ancient** Europe. An **emperor** said young men could not get married. He wanted the men to become **soldiers** instead.

Learn more here!

But people still fell in love. They wanted to marry each other. They thought the emperor was being unfair.

A man named Valentine helped people marry in **secret**. The emperor did not know.

Chapter 3

St. Valentine

The emperor discovered what Valentine was doing. He put Valentine in jail to punish him. Valentine died on February 14.

Learn more here!

Many people were grateful to Valentine. He became known as St. Valentine.

> Valentine's Day is celebrated on the **anniversary** of Valentine's death.

Chapter 4

Celebrations

To celebrate Valentine's Day, people spend time with loved ones. People do nice things for each other.

Complete an activity here!

People often celebrate Valentine's Day by giving small gifts. These gifts may be candy or paper cards.

The gifts are often shaped like hearts. People also decorate with hearts.

The gifts people give each other are called valentines.

Making Connections

Text-to-Self

Have you ever celebrated Valentine's Day? How would you like to celebrate it?

Text-to-Text

Have you read any other books about holidays? What did you learn?

Text-to-World

Valentine's Day is a day to celebrate love. In what ways do you see people sharing love and kindness in the world?

Glossary

ancient – from a long time ago.

anniversary – recognition of a date on which something important happened.

emperor – a leader of a country or group of countries.

secret – something that people do not know about.

soldier – a person who fights in wars.

Index

candy, 4, 20

cards, 4, 20

emperor, 8, 11–12, 14

hearts, 4, 21

love, 4, 6, 11, 18

marriage, 8, 11–12

soldiers, 8

Valentine, 12, 14, 17

Online Resources

popbooksonline.com

Thanks for reading this Cody Koala book!

Scan this code* and others like it in this book, or visit the website below to make this book pop!

popbooksonline.com/valentines-day

*Scanning QR codes requires a web-enabled smart device with a QR code reader app and a camera.